THE SOUL CONNECTION

Production: Sadie Cook
Cover Design: xheight design limited
Published 1999

Respect the legal rights of
your fellow musicians!

DON'T BE
A MUSIC
COPYCAT!

The copying of © copyright
material is a criminal offence
and may lead to prosecution.

IMP

International
MUSIC
Publications

B.A.B.Y.

Words and Music by
Isaac Hayes and David Porter

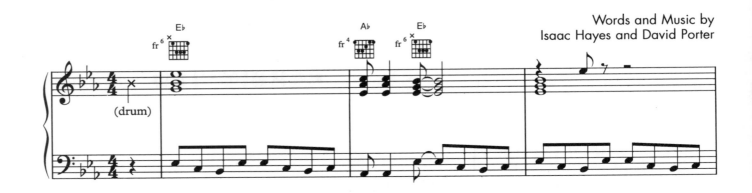

(drum)

(1.) Ba - - by, oh ba - by I
(2.) by, oh ba - by you
(3.) by, oh ba - by you

love to call you ba - by ba - by oh_____ ba –
look so good to me ba - by ba - by oh_____ ba –
look so good to me ba - by ba - by oh_____ ba –

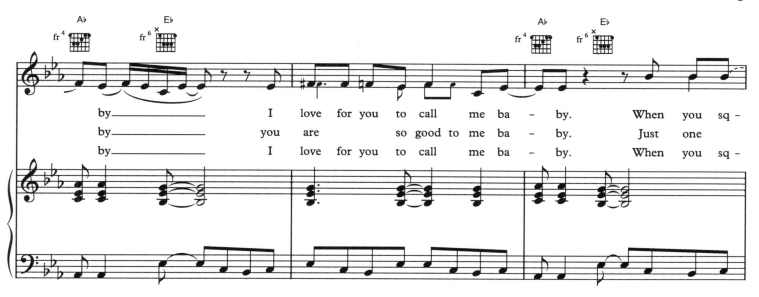

by_____ I love for you to call me ba - by. When you sq-
by_____ you are so good to me ba - by. Just one
by_____ I love for you to call me ba - by. When you sq-

ueeze_____ me re - al tight_____ you know you make the wrong things right_____
look_____ in your eyes_____ and my tem - per - a - ture goes sky high.
ueeze_____ me re - al tight_____ you know you make the wrong things right_____

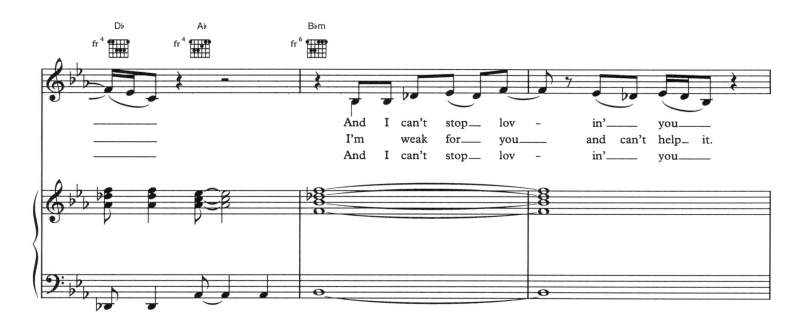

_____ And I can't stop_ lov - in'_____ you_____
_____ I'm weak for_ you_____ and can't help_ it.
_____ And I can't stop_ lov - in'_____ you_____

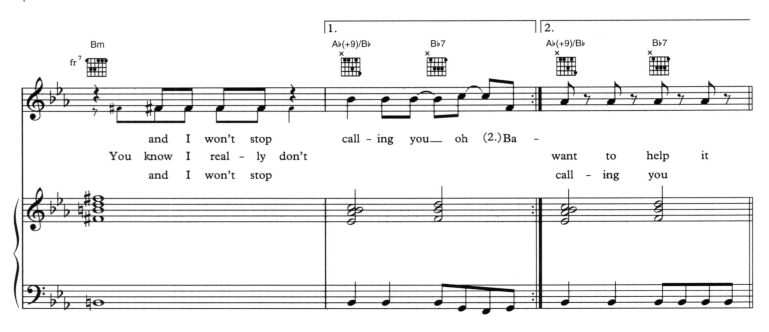

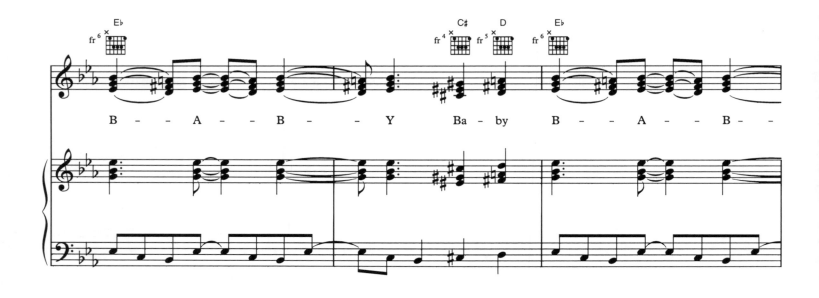

you throw out the life line, then I get real close to you and

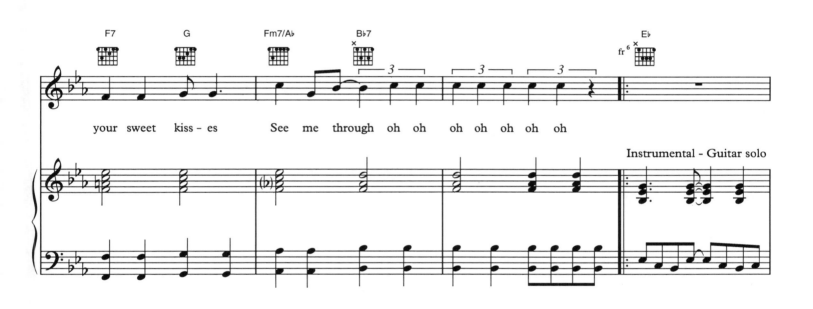

your sweet kiss- es See me through oh oh oh oh oh oh oh

Instrumental - Guitar solo

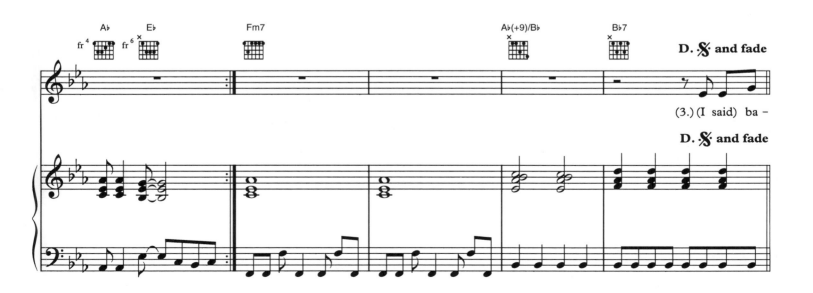

D. %: and fade

(3.) (I said) ba -

D. %: and fade

Chain Of Fools

Words and Music by Donald Covay

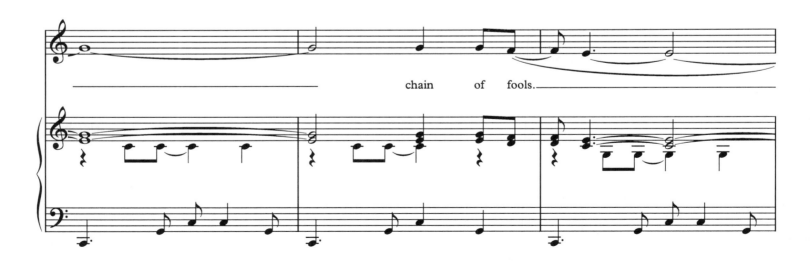

For five long years— I thought you— were my man,

But I found out love,— I'm just a link in your chain.—

You got me where you want me. I ain't no-thin' but your fool.—

You treat-ed me mean,— You treat-ed me cruel.

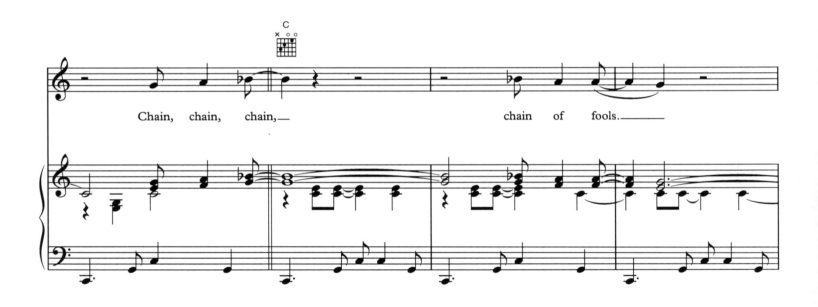

Chain, chain, chain,— chain of fools.—

E-ve-ry chain_____ has got a weak link.—

I may be weak, yeah, but I'll bear the strain.

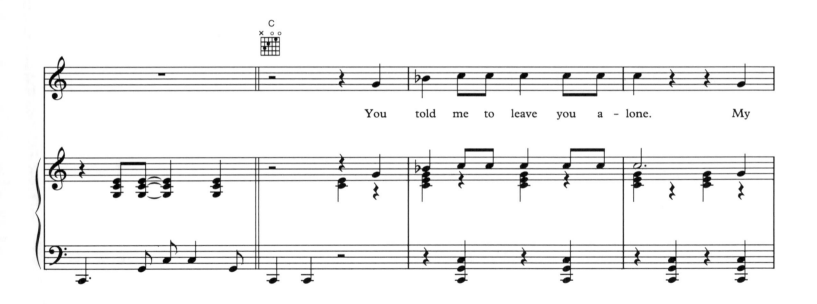

You told me to leave you a - lone. My

fa - ther said come on home.___ My doc - tor said take it ea - sy, oh, but your

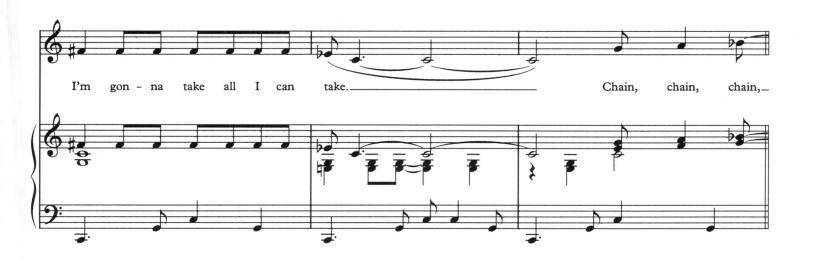

I'm gon - na take all I can take._____ Chain, chain, chain,__

C

_____ chain, chain, chain,_____ chain, chain, chain,

repeat and fade

_____ chain of fools._____ chain, chain, chain,

repeat and fade

The Greatest Love Of All

Words by Linda Creed
Music by Michael Masser

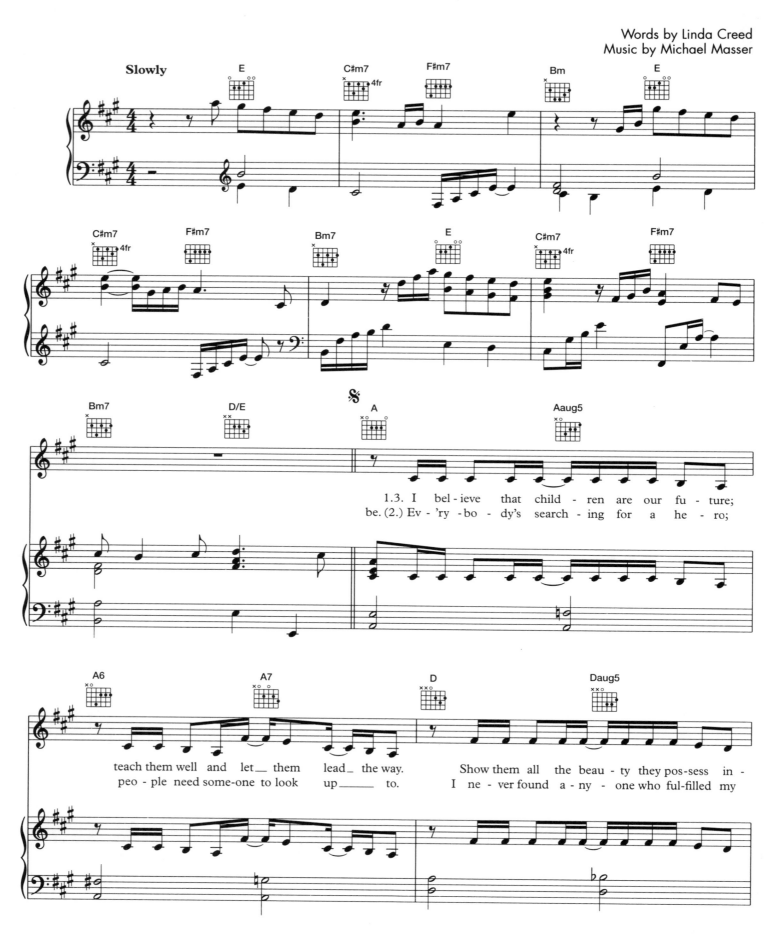

The House That Jack Built

Words and Music by
Bob Lance and Fran Robins

Moderately

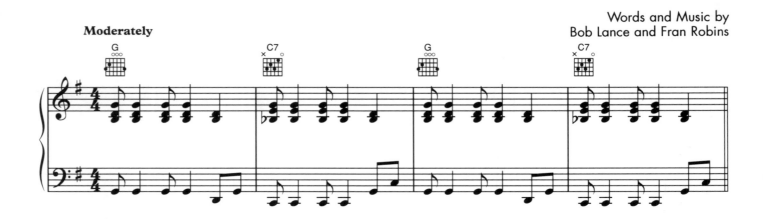

This was the land— that he worked by hand, it was the dream for an up-right man,
There was a fence— that held our love, there was a gate— that he walked out of.

there was a room— that was filled with love, it was the love— that I walked out of.
This is a heart— and it turned to stone, this is a house, it ain't no home.

In The Midnight Hour

Words and Music by
Stephen Cropper and Wilson Pickett Jnr

I'm gon - na

wait 'till the mid - night hour,___ that's when my love comes tum - bl - in' down.
wait 'till the stars come out___ and see that sweet love in___ your eyes.

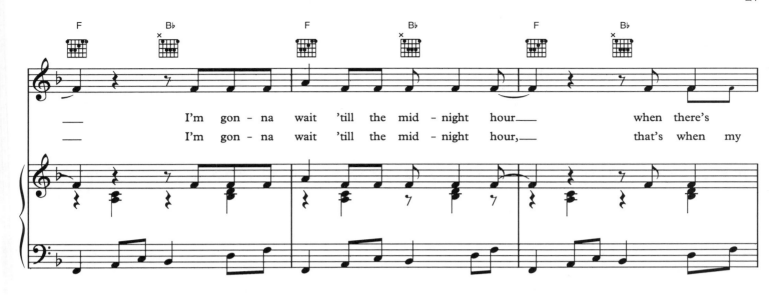

I'm gon - na wait 'till the mid - night hour___ when there's
I'm gon - na wait 'till the mid - night hour,___ that's when my

no - one else a - round.___ I'm gon - na take you___ girl and
love be - gins to shine.___ You're the on - ly___ girl I

hold you, and do all the things I told___ you in the mid - night hour.
know that real - ly___ loves me so,___ in the mid - night hour.

Knock On Wood

Words and Music by
Stephen Cropper and Eddie Lee Floyd

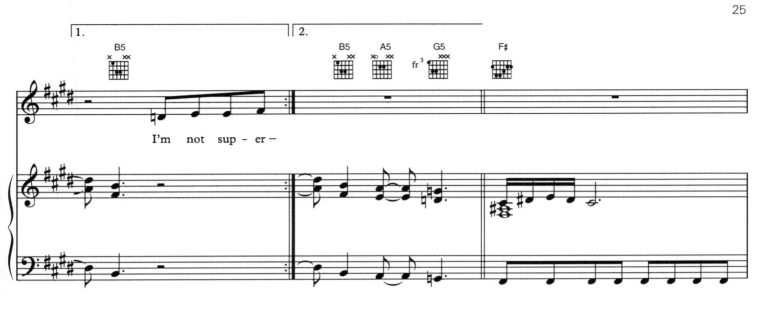

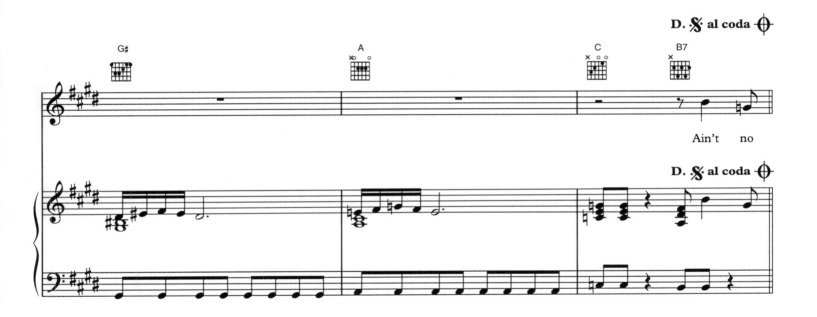

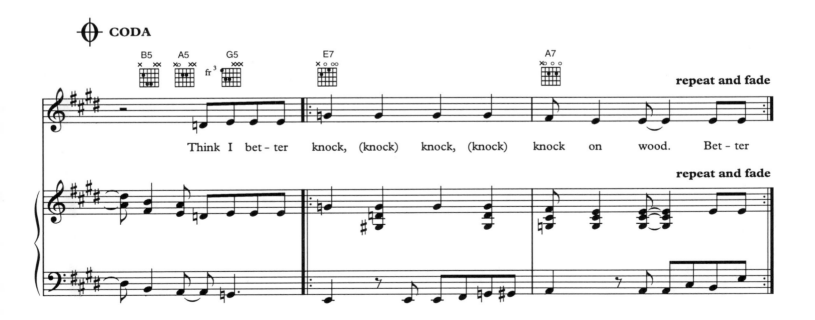

Respect

Words and Music by Otis Redding

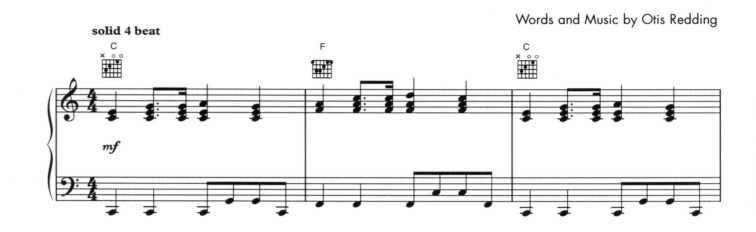

What you want ba-by I got.
I ain't gon-na do you wrong while you gone.

What you need you know I got it.
I ain't gon-na do you wrong 'cause I don't wan-na.

All I as-kin'

is for a lit-tle re - spect, when you come home.   Ba — by,   when you come home,

— re - spect.   I'm out__ to give you   all   my mon - ey,
                                 Ooh,___ your kiss - es,   sweeter than hon - ey,

but all I'm ask - in'   in re - turn, hon - ey   is to give me
but guess__ what,   so here's my   mon - ey,   all I want you to do for me

my pro - per re - spect when you get home.   Yeah,   ba - by,   when   you   get

is give me some here when you get home.   Yeah,   ba - by,   when   you   get

home.   R- E- S- P- E- C- T,   find out what it means to me,

home.

R- E- S- P- E- C- T,   take out T C P,   a lit-tle re -spect.

repeat and fade

Respect Yourself

Words and Music by
Mack Rice and Luther Ingram

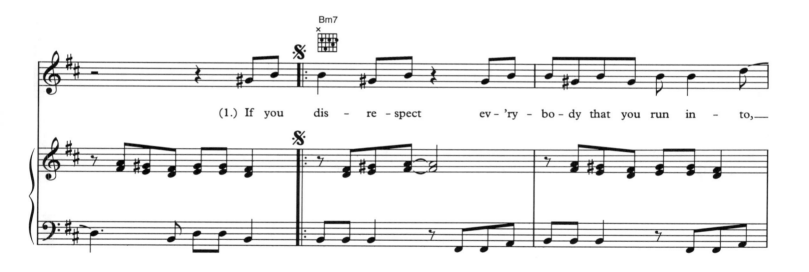

(1.) If you dis-re-spect ev-'ry-bo-dy that you run in-to,

ah now what do you think a-ny-

self ain't no – bo – dy gon – na give a good ca – hoot. Re –

spect your – self,___ re – spect your – self,___ re –

spect your – self,___ re – spect your – self.___ If you're

VERSE 2:
If you don't give a heck
About the man with the Bible in his hand
Just get out the way
And let the gentleman do his thing

VERSE 3:
You're the kind of gentleman
Who's got everything your way
Take the sheet off your face boy,
It's a brand new day.

VERSE 4:
If you're walking around thinking
That the world owes you something 'cause you're here
You're going out the world backwards
Like you did when you first come here.

VERSE 5:
Keep talking about the present
It won't stop evolution
Put your hand on your mouth
When you call, that'll help the solution.

VERSE 6:
Oh you're fussin' round womenfolk
And don't even know their name
Then you come and lock the fate
That'll make you a big hole there.

See-Saw

Words and Music by
Donald Covay and Steve Cropper

Some - times you love me like a good wo - man ought-
tell me I'm your sweet can - dy man,

- a, some - times you hurt me so bad,___
___ then some - times ba - by

see - saw babe, go up, down, all a - round like a see-saw.

1.

C

2.

C   C#7

Some - times you

When I'm kiss - ing you and I

F#m

like it   and ask you to kiss me a - gain,_____ I

(Sittin' On) The Dock Of The Bay

Words and Music by
Otis Redding and Steve Cropper

Soul Man

Words and Music by
Isaac Hayes and David Porter

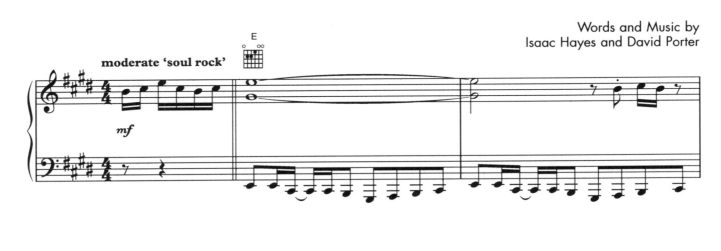

grab your rope and I'll pull you in.___ give you hope and

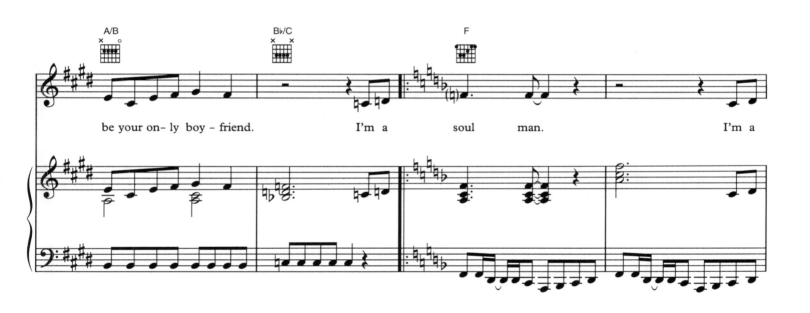

be your on- ly boy - friend. I'm a soul man. I'm a

soul man. I'm a

Take Me To The River

Words and Music by
Al Green and Mabon Lewis Hodges

(1.) I don't know why I love you like I do,___ af-ter all the chan-ges that

(2.) I don't know why she treat-ed me so bad.___ af-ter all the things___ that

(3.) I don't know why I love you like I do,___ af-ter all the things___ that

Take me to the ri – ver, wash me down,

want to cleanse my — soul, — get my feet — on the ground.

Hold me, love — me, please me,

tease me,   till I___   can't   till I can't___   can't take___ no more.

Take me to the   ri – ver.

D.S. repeat chorus ad lib. to fade

D.S. repeat chorus ad lib. to fade

Under The Boardwalk

Words and Music by
Art Resnick and Kenny Young

When A Man Loves A Woman

Words and Music by
Calvin Lewis and Andrew Wright

Without You

Words and Music by
Peter Ham and Tom Evans

No, I can't for-get this eve-ning, or your

face as I was leav-ing but I guess that's just the way the sto-ry

goes. You al-ways smile but in your eyes your sor-row

International Music Publications Limited

England: Griffin House
161 Hammersmith Road
London W6 8BS

Germany: Marstallstrasse 8
D-80539 München

Denmark: Danmusik
Vognmagergade 7
DK-1120 Copenhagen K

Italy: Nuova Carisch Srl.
Via Campania, 12
(Zona industriale Sesto Ulteriano)
20098 San Giuliano Milanese
Milano

Spain: Nueva Carisch Espana, S.L.
Magallanes 25
28015 Madrid

France: Carisch France, SARL
20, rue de la Ville-l'Eveque
75008 Paris

WARNER BROS. PUBLICATIONS U.S. INC.

USA: 15800 N.W. 48th Avenue
Miami, Florida 33014

Australia: 3 Talavera Road
North Ryde
New South Wales 2113

Scandinavia: P.O. Box 533
Vendevagen 85 B
S-182 15 Danderyd
Sweden